Brexit: Aftermath What is the Way Forward.

Written By
Elina Salajeva

To all decision makers; remember fortune favours the brave!

CHAPTER ONE

Contents

Why now Britain want to withdraw from the EU?
Problems with the EU.
Rise of Refugees and the threat of terrorism
The fragility of the Euro.
Britain want independence from the EU laws and rules but will also benefit if they remain as trading partners.
Using the EU's contributory budget to address other issues rather than paying the EU.
Government will be able to take back control of the decision-making process.
Introduction: What is Brexit?
A Brief history of EEC/EU.
Why the EEC or EU: Their Objectives.
What are the advantages of EEC/EU membership?
Increased trading in a tax-free single market.
Easy access to suppliers and Buyers.
Catalyst and springboard between member states and the rest of the world.
Increased and easy investment opportunities from any member state.
Plenty and ease of access to labour resources.
Good quality products and services and increased competition.
The benefits outweigh the cost in terms of membership budget contribution.
The benefits outweigh the cost in terms of membership budget contribution.
Peace and increased cooperation between member's states and encouragement of diversity and linguistic.
What are the disadvantages of EEC/EU membership?

Cost.

Problems of having a single currency the Euro.

Unworkable inefficient policies.

Problems of net migration.

Reduced democracy and more bureaucracy.

Communication barrier as there is no single language among its member states.

Control from central no local government decision making powers.

What are the advantages of remaining in the EU once a member state?

Jobs

Guaranteed benefits derived from trade.

Exports.

Reduced prices of goods among member states.

Improved living standards, human rights and justice and cleaner environment.

The EU as a controller and intermediary to curb and bring big multinational companies to justice.

Plenty of opportunities for any single country's inhabitants throughout the EU.

Integration, cooperation and peace.

Better working standards and improved pay and working conditions.

Technological research and development.

A single point of control.

Loss of the hard work achieved over the years, loss of allies and power to influence future decisions.

What are the disadvantages of remaining in the EU once a member state?

Cost on membership fees.

Too many laws that hinder individual member's progress.

Continued lack of government control.

Lack of proper control of immigration.

Continued lack of proper security.

Most now see the EU as undemocratic and out of date.

Threat of a lack of future independence and military freedom.

Continued lack of fiscal control in the future when faced with economic hardships.

Why Britain joined the EU did it have anything to do with helping the economy? An overview.

Examples from other countries that have withdrawn their European Union membership.

The case of Greenland.

The case of Algeria.

What are the impacts of leaving the EU to the remaining EU block?

Destabilization of the EU and possibility of a chain reaction.

Britain government's views and position in the period leading to the referendum.

A look at the prime minister's stance before the referendum.

Immigration as a point of renegotiating the EU membership.

Delegating decision making powers to London rather than Brussels.

Free trade and the ability to make own fiscal policies.

Free trade and the ability to make own fiscal policies.

The other point regarded free trade and competition within the single market.

Rejection of a single military army.

Can Britain re hold the referendum in order to stay in the EU?

Are there any laws to overrule the referendum results and what can Britain do to remain in the EU if need be?

Situation before Article 50 of the Lisbon treaty is invoked.

A look at the economy.

Foreign Investment.

Situation 2 years after implementation of Article 50 of the Lisbon Treaty.

EU- Canada deal.

The EU-South Korean deal.

Transatlantic Trade and Investment Agreement (TTI)between EU and America.

Complete exit without any more special ties with the EU. Scenario One.

Possible trade deals with India, China, Canada and the US.

Exit from the EU but with some renegotiated trade deals.

The Third Scenario: The UK has only a customs agreement with the EU.

Article 50 of the Lisbon treaty.

Situation 5years after implementation of Article 50 of the Lisbon Treaty.

Situation 10 years after implementation of Article 50 of the Lisbon Treaty.

What is the future of the EU post Britain?

Will Britain join again the EU in the future and what will be likely impact of such a move.

Why would Britain want to join the EU again in the future?

Dealing with the aftermath shock if uncontrolled that will result in a recession.

Political threats from other countries.

Overview

The people of Britain have voted; they have decided that now it's time to take the next step through the development process. There are old enough and mature enough to take the next step through life, and become as independent and self-sufficient as ever. They think they have been trained enough and have acquired the necessary skills and training they needed. The training is over, they cannot be guided now, they are like an 18year old, suddenly you are on your own, parental guidance is over, now you are expected to live your own life like a full grown up. All these years you been under the protection of your parents, guiding you, telling you what you should do and not do. Your parents have shown you the way, protected you when you struggled, corrected your mistakes whenever you failed, they had defended you when you were in trouble. They had shown you how to live your life. They had protected you when you needed help, they have paid all your debts, they have shown you how to live with the others, your brothers and sisters in the house. Even when you were wrong they have shown you love and guided you. When your brothers and sisters argued with you, they had been to your rescue, they had negotiated on your behalf. Everything you needed they had worked hard to make sure that you got it. They had looked for places of school for you, they had gone there in advance, negotiated with the principle of the school or the headmaster on your behalf so that you have the best time at school. They have never done anything which was not in your interest, all their work is to make sure you have the best life has to offer. They have gone out of their way for you and in return all they ask from you, is your loyalty and love towards them.

But you are now 18 years old and the past years are now like a fairytale story, is this ever going to be forever? As time goes by you are also growing up, you are becoming more and more mature, you have been guided over the years now it's time you stand up on your own feet without their help. Your parents cannot be there for you forever you know. There comes a time when you must manage your own life, your own affairs. You are 18 years now? What does this mean?

First you can no longer rely on your parents for everything. You have to take that initial step and start providing for yourself, start thinking about your future. Your parents were there for you all your life, now all of a sudden you realize that you are 18 and things can never be the same again. What's the first feelings you have experienced the time you become independent from your parents? For most I think it's mixed feelings? First it's fear, oh my God, how am I going to pull this through on my own? I have never done this before? On the other hand, you could be jumping up and down in the air with excitement? Woo, I am a man now, I am a woman now, whatever your situation is!

You look at your best friend America or if it's a girl, Americally next door. He or she is 18 as well and probably younger than you with months between you and his or her birthday.

Damn!! You say to yourself. He or she has never been guided by her parents all her life but damn he or she is doing just fine.

You realize that you are actually in a better position, you have been shown how life works, you have more immediate friends and help around you than most of your friends.

Now it's time to take the next step in life, although no one said it was easy, but deep down you know this is the only way. If America or Americally your best friend can do it alone, why can't I? You ask yourself.

This time you approach your parents and ask for permission to move out of the family house after 2 months. Your dad Franco and your mother Germaine goes ballistic on hearing this. "Are you out of your mind?", exclaimed your dad. Deep down he knows it's time for you to stand on your own, but when you are gone and doing things by yourself he will realize that his life will be empty. He worked so hard and you are the reason for his existence, every time you said thank you, he felt good about himself and wanted to do more for you. But the big question is that, will he forever be there for you. If you don't start now when are you going to start? Will time wait for you? What will happen that time when he is old and can't even support himself? Your mum has shown you much love over the years, she had sacrificed her own life to be there for you, it's her maternal duty, she feels she must guide you, she feels it's her duty to protect you, after all you needed the help anywhere. All her life she has tried to guide you and support you. She has been everywhere on your behalf advocating for you and acting as a catalyst on your behalf. You have everything you need because of her. But she even knows that, time waits for no man, one day you have to stand on your own two legs. She doesn't want you to move out of the family house, because you are her child, she tries to talk you out of it. But deep down you realize that it's time to take that first step, you insist that you need to move out of the family house, it's time you do it alone.

The big question I would like to ask is this, is Britain in the same scenario to an 18year old? For argument sack and this being my own opinion which is subjective, I think I would like to say yes to some extent. Please don't dismiss the idea too early because a closer look at the situation or the picture I am trying to portray, will help you understand the way forward for Britain in the future. These are my own ideas and no offense is intended and I could be wrong but I think it's worth trying to understand the principle behind this. I have used this comparison or notion of the EU as parents in order for you to understand the implications of any action to be taken in the future. The EU has acted as a parent to all other EU members, with Germany and France as the super-states of the EU. The EU has been a catalyst in negotiations and has acted as a springboard for the member states in securing favorable deals around the world, all which benefits its member states. It has acted on behalf of everyone to set up laws and rules and to make sure that everyone follows these, in order to stabilize the establishment and for all to work as one unit with the same goal, at the same time maintaining peace and development. The EU has been relentless trying to secure deals with America through the establishment of the Transatlantic Trade and Investment deal. They are in talks with Canada negotiating the Comprehensive Economic and Trade Agreements (CETA). They have secured the EU-South Korea deal, the Singapore-EU deal, among others. The EU has made it easy for member states to access world markets and boost each members' development and growth.

On June 23 2016 the British people held a referendum in which the majority voted to leave the EU. The main reasons being that Britain wants to be a sovereign state once again, they no longer want the EU to dictate what to do or what not to do. The British government now want to make their laws and regulations; they want powers to make their own decisions. They want to be able to control their borders and to decide who should and should not come to Britain. They want to impose restrictions on what benefits are available to EU members and how long the EU members should be in the country to get the benefits.

The British government now want to manage their own finances; they want the Bank of England to be able to set interest rates that are suitable to them. They want to control how they will deal with a financial crisis in the future, they no longer want the EU to set limits to the amount they can borrow in case of a recession. In short the British government is advocating for the ability to make their own economic and fiscal policies that are specific to Britain.

The feelings in Brussels especially among Germany and France, the two EU super-states, is that of anger and dismay with Britain. They feel let down by Britain, they want to take a hard stance when dealing with Britain, they want to set it as an example. The main reason being that Britain's exit might set a series of small tsunamis that can destabilize and threaten the existence of the EU. They don't want to witness a chain reaction which they might be unable to control. Their point is that, now that Britain has insisted on leaving the EU, they want Britain out, and they are urging London to invoke article 50 as soon as possible. Their main concern is that any delay and uncertainty will not be good for the EU economy. The leaders in Brussels want Britain out without any renegotiations, they have hinted that it will not be fair to cherry pick their policies as what Britain is trying to do. If you want to be a member then you must abide by the rules and regulations of the EU, you cannot cherry pick what you think is best for you and choose to ignore other regulations. The British had refused to adopt the euro as part of their membership. The EU leadership believes that the EU was formed with the idea of a single market, a market with the same currency and free movement of people, goods and services. The only way to stimulate growth and development is for every member state to follow and implement the rules and regulations, to use the single euro currency and to allow free movement of goods and services. Some EU leaders have argued that Britain with its rejection of using the euro was frustrating growth and development and it was not easy for the EU to realize its full potential.

Britain has realized that although they had benefited over the years by being in the EU, now it's time they do it alone. The EU has been very helpful in the initial years, with easy access to labour, biggest market and resources, it has managed to stabilize its declining economy since joining in 1973. The EU has increased the British exports since Britain joined, by providing ready markets in 27 different countries. The EU is the major contributor of British foreign investment. Britain has a balance of payments deficit and the EU has provided needed direct foreign investment to offset this balance of payments. Looking at last year alone 44% of exports from Britain went to the EU worth about £229bn. To offset its balance of payments, Britain relies on direct foreign investment from the EU. Britain has in the past been a hot spot for investment mainly because, first, it is part of the EU, secondly it has a good rule of law, thirdly it is an English-speaking country which is universal and lastly it has a well-educated population. Recently there has been a continuous fall in direct investment that partly explains the continuous balance of payment deficit. The big question is, why? Firstly, and foremost a continuous balance of payment deficit is a sign of the country's uncompetitiveness, which will lead to lower economy growth and prospects in the future. In case where capital and financial flows ceases it is easy for the exchange rate to depreciate and living standards will fall in the long run. Thirdly it means the economy is not balanced either we are importing more than we are exporting. So, the big question is why this deficit and what are the implications?

Here I will look at the trade between Britain and the EU. First we are buying more goods from the EU than we are exporting to them. This is not surprising because Britain has de-industrialized and we are more of a service nation. We import more products from the EU than we export to them. This is in part explained by the stagnate economies of the EU. There have been high unemployment levels in the EU and a lot of problems associated with the euro. Spending incomes of the EU members have declined over the years. The EU has seen a lot of crisis with the Greek crises and the need for bailout in countries like Ireland, Portugal and Spain. All this has meant that the buying power of EU members has been declining over the years. Their economies are stagnating. Would you rather stay in the EU and deal with stagnating economies or you would like to make trade deals with emerging fast growing markets like in India, China and the rest of the world? Britain if it exits the EU it will be able to make trade deals with countries with high spending powers and growing economies that will boost its exports of goods and services.

Looking at the EU, they have been spearheading growth and development in the 70's to the early 2000 years. Over the recent years the EU has been plagued by a lot of problems. The costs now outweigh the benefits, there is too much red tape and bureaucracy. Their policies have stifled growth and development especially of small to medium sized companies. To spearhead the British economy Britain must exit the EU as a member and form deals as a partner just like other major countries like South Korea, the US, Canada.

Britain should think like an 18year old who has been given independence and freedom to choose the course of action in life and seek to establish partnerships with the rest of the world and especially with the EU but on a different capacity.

At the current moment Britain is within the EU which means under the protection of the EU, when it should be side by side with the EU like the US, South Korea or Canada. This is very very important as it will detect the success or failure of Britain in the future. Now, there are growing fears that Britain might struggle and be left out in the cold if it exits the EU, I personally think that these fears are unfounded. You cannot remain under the guidance of your parents forever, so Britain and its people must look at this situation in the same way, come thunder or rain. The EU if you look at it considering the above paradigm of an 18-year-old, has acted like a parent protecting its young ones from the outside world. No member can be expected to grow more the EU itself, so all these rules and regulations are there to see to it that, that will be the case. No wonder they have been so many problems in recent years. The EU is there to offer you protection, it's existence is to offer protection and to guide you. In other words, it's for those who need protection, it' for companies that need protection, companies in infancy stages that would otherwise struggle in the real world if they are not protected. It's for helping countries that would otherwise not make it on their own.

Is Britain such a country that need protection and that must be guided? Or Britain is like one of the big boys, like America, like South Korea, like Canada? Boys who would rather be a partner to the EU rather than be under the EU.

Looking at British past years and its dealings with the EU then EEC, Charles de Gaulle the then French president had put some insight into the British people but it all had fallen on deaf ears. Some 53 years ago this wise guy had insisted that Britain was already an independent big boy who is free and able to run his own affairs and therefore joining the EU was like liking to go back into your mother's womb years after birth. He refused the UK to join the EU. Clearly there was no need for Britain to join the EU, the EU only accommodated those who need protection and Britain was not one of the country. In 1967 Britain insisted that it needed protection and again this general stressed out that such protection was not meant for the strong and able bodied but for the weak, those who had been ravaged by war, those who had been traumatized seeing and witnessing the war and poverty with whose industries and agriculture needed protection.

A quick look at the reasons cited by Charles de Gaulle the French president at the time for refusing Britain to join the EU.

In De Gaulle's very words:

"England in effect is insular, she is maritime, she is linked through her exchanges, her markets, her supply lines to the most diverse and often the most distant countries; she pursues essentially industrial and commercial activities, and only slight agricultural ones. She has in all her doings very marked and very original habits and traditions"

Wikipedia

Clearly the French president highlighted that the British had little agricultural activity and they would not benefit by joining the EEC. The EEC was mainly an agricultural and fisheries community, because of this he was skeptical about the reason why Britain wanted to join.

50 years down the line the British people had realized that they have no gains from joining and wanted out. The French president saw that Britain was independent and its agriculture successful it didn't need any protection then. The EEC was to help countries that were struggling to protect its companies and industries. According to reports it seemed the UK had initially rejected Charles de Gaulle's proposal to join the EEC in favor of making allies with the US. When France and Germany's economies started to grow then the UK changed their position and decided to join the EEC which was met with skepticism by the then French president. Probably the French president viewed the UK as a Trojan horse for the US. Their economic position was strong and needed not join the EEC. The French president saw UK's stance as there to weaken the EEC and frustrate progress and to represent America's interests. He assumed Britain had a political agenda rather than an economic one, Germany and France's economies

were gathering momentum and these countries were a threat to peace and security. German and France's growth had nothing to do with the EEC, the growth was due to individual's states' effort to stimulating growth through injection of money into the economy. EU policy had always been irrelevant to the economic growth of individual states. At the time Britain had high defense spending overseas that led to continuous balance of payment crises and this balance of payment crises had nothing to do with the fact that Britain was not a member of the EU then EEC.

Having looked at the above reasons for rejection it seemed the generals view was skewed, certainly Britain is and was not a puppet of the Americans. Britain had simply foreseen the economic and political opportunities presented by joining the EEC. Britain had seen itself as independent and needed not be governed by the EEC.

Britain joined the EEC because joining was perceived as a way to stop its relative economic decline. Britain's per capita GDP was a third larger than all the EEC member states in the 1950s. At the time of joining Britain's per capita was now 10% below that of all EEC members. Joining the EEC has stabilized its per capita GDP since joining the EEC.

Although joining the EU has meant a stable economy, Britain should be ambitious and take the first step to achieve greater economic growth. They say fortune favours the brave, it's time to stop depending on the EU and take a bold step in becoming more independent like other countries outside the EU. The idea now is to consider establishing partnership relationships with the EU than as subordinate ones. Britain's friend, America is not bound by EU's rules and obligations but they are trying to formulate a mutually agreement as equal partners to boost both their economies.

No to subordination but more emphasis on partnerships, must be written on the forehead of every British decision maker. Britain is a rich country in terms of the rule of the law, a highly educated labour force, the use of English and all these factors are factors that can contribute to the success of the country. Being in the EU will and has been slowing growth and development. No to socialism, the idea should be that of a free market, where markets are not controlled but where they are free. Although some controls and regulations are needed here and there, the extent and length depends on the stages of development the country is in.

It's time for Britain to be ambitious and to take the bull by the horns and start viewing any problems as stepping stones to a successful Britain. (NB I think you should read my other book: Chase your dreams never give up).

Ok having looked at the above background to the issues to be addressed later it's time to address some fears and current misconceptions regarding Brexit.

Firstly, I think Britain should take this opportunity to try and negotiate a deal with the EU as a partner rather than the current situation as a subordinate of the EU. The threat of exiting the EU can give them a bargaining advantage. This should be a way forward, Britain should try and think independently and start viewing the EU as a partner like other countries like the US, South Korea and Canada. Britain should no longer be a subordinate of the EU but a partner. They should negotiate as partnership and secure better deals with the EU. The idea is to take all its opportunities because the road ahead is tough but walkable. If Britain cannot be partners with the EU, then the other option is to form other partnerships and make deals with the rest of the world. Britain need access to the single market, there is no doubt about that, the EU's bargaining power is formidable but Britain has passed that stage where it's a subordinate, it can only be in a partnership with the EU and not under it.

In order to see the problems at hand and the issues that need to be addressed I will look at the reasons Britain want to exit the euro now, and this will pave the way for a solution or approach that is likely to be adopted or rather which they should adopt as a way forward.

Why now Britain want to withdraw from the EU?

Problems with the EU.

The EU is now seen as robbing other countries of their money, their sovereignty, their identity and their democracy. Currently the EU faces a wide range of problems mainly slow growth and high unemployment like in member states like Greece and Spain. The EU is threatened by the rise of populist political movements which are anti-EU. There are several factors that has seen a sharp rise of anti-EU movements. The poor handling of the Greek crises, immigration and refugee crises, the resurgent of Russia and heightened terrorist threat from within the EU zone. The 2008-2009 recession and the euro zone debt crisis hugely affected European countries with rising unemployment and huge debts. Some countries needed assistance from the EU, countries like Portugal, Ireland and Greece, but even after the austerity measures they still had high unemployment rates and huge debt, with slow growth and high inflation with social unrest.

There has been a rise in populist movements that are anti-EU in recent years. The main argument of disapproval of the EU is that national sovereign has been lost due to too much control from Brussels. Those unhappy with EU points to the lack of leadership and future vision of the EU. Some point out that too much power resides with Germany alone, in the light of dealing with the Greek crisis, dealing with Russian aggression and the migration and refugee crisis in recent years. There are divisions and mistrust within EU members considering the Greece crises. France and Germany disagreed on the best ways to deal with the crises, that saw divisions emerging. There have always been other disagreements when dealing with fiscal austerity measures and ways to increase growth. Member states are arguing now that some countries like Germany are now putting more emphasis on country interest that with the EU as in the past. Britain is now seeking independence from the EU, there are too many problems associated with the EU now. Too much red tape and bureaucracy and Britain can do without the EU, it's time to take that first step, and do it alone.

Rise of Refugees and the threat of terrorism.

In recent years, there has been many terrorist activities for example the Paris attacks of 2015 and the bombings in Brussels. Most of the terrorists were Europeans with Syrian and Iraqi's origin but now residing in Europe. The Islamic state is increasing the threat of terrorism every day. Although the EU has responded swiftly to the threat of terrorism by increasing information sharing among members and the EU authorities strengthening external border controls, the threat is still there posed by the

Islamic state and other home grown groups who are often to and from the conflicts zones in Syria and Iraq.

There has been a rise of migrants from the war-torn zones of Syria, Afghanistan and the poverty stricken past of Asia and Africa that has put enormous pressure on the EU. The wars and poverty have created a wave of people from other countries coming to the EU. The resultant EU strategies to combat and accommodate this rise in migration was unsuccessful. The EU was not prepared for any influx of immigrants from middle east origin. The EU lacked effective and proper plans to deal with the refugee crises as they failed to deal with a large influx of refugees from outside the EU. This refugee crises created deep divisions among member states, some member states were not prepared to accommodate the refugees from Greece and Syria for example. They pointed out that their infrastructure could not handle the refugees. Hence there were divisions as to how many refugees each country can accommodate and what sort of support and assistance financially, each country would get from the EU. The EU's redistribution and resettlement programs were highly unsuccessful and were received with much controversy. There were fears of security which the EU failed to address, most of the dispersed refugees were non-Christians, and most member states have dominantly Christian communities. The refugees were Muslims, and such a move has been seen to increase social tensions and threatens security which is a fundamental principle or cornerstone on which the EU was founded. There has been fears of future problems in terms of social cohesion and terrorism. Considering the free movement of people within the EU member states some member states argued that this move would weaken their boundaries. There will be no way of controlling migration and thereby this will increase terrorism. Some countries are now seeing this as one of the weaknesses of the modern EU. The modern EU formerly a Christian and peaceful group of different countries will become a multi faith establishment. This has increased fears of social unrest and tension between the recent Muslim refugees and the local Christian groups. With no border controls, attack is imminent and because of this many members are reconsidering their membership. Britain put the security of its people foremost, the EU is not changing with the times. Ten years ago, ok, it was ideal to be in the EU, now it's a different story. When it comes to security, any country would want to act fast, no one wants to be a seating duck. It's an undisputed fact, that the recent migration to the European Union from Syria and Afghanistan has to some extent increased the risk of terrorism, although I would like to emphasis that refugees are in no way linked to terrorists. My point is that terrorists might take the same route as refugees to enter the European union. Considering this the EU, is changing things can no longer be the same, governments must try and think about protecting their borders and their people. Britain is no different, they must act as well. The cornerstone of the EU, that of free movement of people, can be a weakness. The has been talks about the EU establishing a military army in response to the increased risk of terrorism and attacks from other countries. Such a move has been seen by Britain as infringing their sovereignty. Britain want to be in control and they want to make decisions themselves, they want to be in control of their military, that way their independence is guaranteed.

Britain want a win-win situation and to get that the only way is to exit the EU and be sovereign, and have the power to make your own decisions and as long as you are in the EU, it will never be a win-win situation, the idea behind the EU is that of protection therefore you have to give and take. This is the main principle behind EU's protection, in other words it's more like scratch my back then I scratch yours. Once Britain and the rest of the EU have realized that, then they will be able to make the right decisions. Taking the proposal put forward by the EU of forming their own military army, that would give the EU members protection against terrorist and any future threats but that will strip them of any sovereign and power. It' a give your freedom or surrender your own military and in return we will defend you. But the big question is, what about tomorrow will EU not use that against them who can predict whats going to happen in the future who can read someone's mind. That raises another question, is it not safe to cover our backs all the time?

The problem most countries are facing with the EU is trying to strike a balance between independence and economic growth. In real-life, once you are in, then you must play by the book, it's never a win-win situation you must be prepared to lose something in return of something else this is the big point often misunderstood. Most government now think that you can cherry pick EU's policies to suit your countries needs which is often a mistake. It's either you are in or not, it can't work both ways it's never going to be a win-win situation no matter what, it will ever be a win-lose or lose-lose situation.

The only way out for those who are not of the faint hearted, for those you want to chase their dreams, those ambitious enough to think outside the box, the only way is out. To hell with being a subordinate it's time to say hello to partnership.

The EU if I am not mistaken has its principles rooted in the socialist movement but is only refined to meet current economic and political climate otherwise the principles are the same.

The main idea behind this is that of dependence, the EU exist because all members are depended on it. Without this dependence, then in theory the EU will cease to exist. So, it's survival is dependent upon you fueling it with request of needing protection, so they take your money and go on your behalf and secure deals for you, ok good deals I must admit, but ask yourself what if I can do it on my own? The is the same notion, and the approach Britain should take. What if I can go and make the same deal myself, although it might not be as good but still one day you might be as good as those who are making the deals for you. Life is about taking chances and I think Britain now that they have the chance to kick start this journey, the EU should be a thing of the past as long as they view Britain as subordinates and not partners. Look at South Korea, it's not in EU, they don't care much about the EU all they want is doing business as partners and still they are trading as partners. The US, soon Canada so why not Britain.

The world is changing and the EU has lacked authority in dealing with countries like Russian when in the case of Ukraine. Russia has resurged on the political platform as a threat to peace and sovereign of the EU as it was supporting separatist insurgence in eastern and southern Ukraine. The EU has imposed sanctions on Russia in order to try and stop it supporting the insurgence who pose threats to the security of the EU. There is concern that

Russia is supporting the populists anti-EU movements which are there to destabilize the EU.

The fragility of the Euro.

Britain is one of the EU members who has refused to use the euro currency. The euro had been associated with high unemployment rates, fiscal problems and recessions. Britain was opposed to the idea of a one size fits all as proposed by the European central bank. Britain wanted to control part of its interest rates which is contradictory to using the use of the euro. Adopting the euro will mean loss of control of all fiscal policies. Adopting the euro would also come into conflict with what the sterling provides, comfort and protection when using the exchange rates. Adopting the euro would mean that Britain must meet the euro convergence criteria which it has failed by almost 80% having only achieved a 20% of maintaining debt to GDP ratio that impacts Britain's fiscal policy. The other reason was that politically it was not favorable to adopt the euro currency by dishing out the sterling. Britain is conservative and would like to remain autonomous and any move to dilute it into EU standards would be met with skepticism politically.

From an economic point of view adopting the euro will mean a loss of monetary and fiscal control which would render England's Monetary Policy Committee (MPC) unimportant. This would mean that the European Central Bank would come up with a one size fits all fiscal policy which might not be suitable for Britain.

If Britain has to join the EU that would mean their interest rates which are above 5% would fall to 2.25% in line with other EU rates. The fall of interest rates would mean problems of inflation and can also affect the housing market. Sensitivity of interest rates means sensitive of the housing market as well. Most UK's people own their houses as they have mortgages unlike their counter parts in Europe. Any change in interest rates by 2% will boost the housing market which will also fuel inflation. Adopting the euro means also loss of fiscal control and independence. The EU limits government borrowing to 3% of Its GDP which means in a recession the country will have problems to kick start recovery.

Britain want independence from the EU laws and rules but will also benefit if they remain as trading partners.
There are no more benefits to be gained from being a member state of the EU. Any benefits to be gained had been gained already, people now argue that it would be beneficial to be independent from the EU but as long as Britain remain as a trading partner. Britain would negotiate a new deal to trade in the single market but without governed by the EU. Other countries like the Swiss and Norway have experienced prosperity outside the EU but still as trading partners. They have renegotiated deals with the EU to continue trading thereby enjoying the benefits of the single market whilst not governed by its laws and regulations. Britain can do the same, other countries like Canada, China and the USA are independent of the EU yet successful. Britain can also forge other trade deals with other non-European countries like New Zealand, India, China, Canada and Australia and still prosper.

Using the EU's contributory budget to address other issues rather than paying the EU.

The EU will spend the contributory fee somewhere else. It was said that Britain give the EU at least £50million a day, that money can be best used for research or development or other pressing needs rather than fund the EU.

Government will be able to take back control of the decision-making process.
The government will be able to tailor make their policies to suit their people and their business and this will boost their economy and future business ventures. The EU is now perceived as undemocratic and there only to serve the big countries that were origin members who seem to make policies that foster their economic development with marginal benefits for other member states.

Introduction: What is Brexit?
Brexit means "Britain exist" from the European Union(EU) after the voting on 23 June 2016.It is an abbreviation of Britain exist. The British people voted for the exit of Britain from EU which they joined on 1 January 1973. A referendum was carried out to gauge the support of the country's continued membership of the European Union, formerly the European Economic Community (EEC). In the June 23 2016 elections the people of Britain voted by 51.9% to leave the EU. There has been other referendum before this one, one of which was held in 1975, with 67% of the voters voting to remain in the EU then EEC.

A Brief history of EEC/EU.
EEC stands for European Economic Community which was a regional organization with the aim of bringing and

stabilizing economic integration and growth between the member states. This was a result of the 1957 Rome treaty. Upon the formation of the European Union(EU) in 1993 the EEC was incorporated as the European Community (EC).

European Union (EU)has its origins in the European coal and steel community and the European Economic Community. It was formed in 1993 as a political and economic partnership of 28 member countries mainly in Europe. It was formed after World War two the reason being that countries who are partners and trade together tend not to fight thereby encouraging political and economic stability. EU was a child birth of German and France, five years after the war ended. It was originally meant to avoid war between these countries and to foster exchange and trade of steel and coal. In 1957 the Rome treaty expanded this original treaty to include other member states. The idea behind this establishment was to make things easy between member states and to foster free movement of goods and people as what happens in one country. The member state region is considered as a one regional development area to encourage economic growth and foster a single market principle where member states can trade and exchange labour freely.

The EU has its own currency which is used by 19 of the member states and has its own rules and laws. There are four key institutions namely the European Commission, the European Parliament, the European Council and the Court of Justice which all are responsible for the running of the EU. The EU budget is around 145bn Euro with every member state contributing to the budget and with Germany being the biggest contributor contributing more than 21% of the budget. Each country gets a rebate towards its contribution and above all each country gets support and money for development and projects.

Why the EEC or EU: Their Objectives.

The EEC was established as a common market with the aim of fostering economic growth and development with the free movement of goods and labour among the trading bloc. It had a lot of objectives from eliminating regional inequalities by fostering growth and development of poorest member states. It aimed to promote human rights and encourage education among its members.

*The other objective was to preserve the environment and to reduce pollution.

*The other objective of the EU was to create an internal market where markets were free and undistorted.

*To encourage sustainable development through economic growth and the stabilization of price.

*To encourage scientific and technological advancement.

*To establish integration and common government among member states

*To promote peace and wellbeing of the it's people

* To establish an area of peace, security and justice among its member states.

*Promoting social, economic and territorial cohesion among member states.

What are the advantages of EEC/EU membership?

Increased trading in a tax-free single market

The 28 member states create a rich single market for any one member country to trade in with an annual value of more than $16trillion with a population of more than 500million. There is tax-free trading which helps reduce prices of goods and food. Other member states benefit from a single market with no tariffs or restrictions. The ability to freely trade and access the market is beneficial to all small and medium businesses. Member states increase their business sales by over 50% because of the EU.

Easy access to suppliers and Buyers.

Member states have free access to suppliers and buyers with EU contributing heavily to exports and imports of the member states. There is easy access of rare and specialized commodities which would have otherwise been difficult or expensive to get if the EU didn't exist.

Catalyst and springboard between member states and the rest of the world.

The EU is not only a single market for member states fostering economic development and sustainability, it is also a springboard for trade and access to the rest of the world. It makes deals with non-member states that benefit the member states. Where necessary some trade agreements between the remainder of the world and the EU members are negotiated, fostered and subsidized by the EU to benefit the member states. The EU is responsible for negotiating up to 30 trade deals with the rest of the world to benefit its members. There are deals with other countries like Canada, Japan and the USA which benefits its members and which any member state would find it difficult to foster on its own.

Increased and easy investment opportunities from any member state.

Membership means increased flow of investment among member states as the countries are free to invest anywhere among member states without any restriction and rules. This in turn encourages economic growth and development among member states. The ability to invest in another EU member state without any restrictions will have a positive impact on investment.

Plenty and ease of access to labour resources.

Free movement of labour among member states has economic benefits as each member state can easily plug skills gaps. This is good for any business as it will be easy to recruit and transfer staff from other member states without any restrictions.

Good quality products and services and increased competition.

The single market means unilateral control and regulations that benefits all member states and benefit consumers as controls and regulations means good quality products throughout member states.

The establishment of a common single market means increased competition and reduced prices and better quality products.

The benefits outweigh the cost in terms of membership budget contribution.

For most member states the budgetary contributions are relatively small as compared to the benefits, in other words the benefits to be gained outweighs the cost. Germany contributes to around 21.3% of the budget followed by France with around 15.7% and Britain around 12.5% of the budget.

Countries that benefit the most by being in the EU are those mainly with huge agricultural and research projects and those with huge economic inequalities this is emphasized by the budget spending plans looking at the 2014-2020 budget. The EU planned to spend 29% of the 2014-2020 960bn Euro budget on agricultural funds for farmers and 13% of the budget on research and training to boost growth. 33% of the funds were put aside to support the poor regions. In total 75% of the budget will benefit member states with huge agricultural developments and economic inequalities.

Peace and increased cooperation between member states and encouragement of diversity and linguistic.
The EU has fostered peace and harmony among member states and has also encouraged diversity as there was no one or common language required. It has encouraged human rights, social justice and upholding of the law.

What are the disadvantages of EEC/EU membership?

Cost
First and foremost, cost of the EU is a disadvantage to member states especially the advanced member states that don't rely on agriculture and development. The cost of EU membership is phenomenon for example Britain's cost of membership is in the region of £15bn gross per year.

Problems of having a single currency the Euro.
The EU emphasize use of a single currency which has seen low rates of economic growth and which has contributed to high unemployment. Some member states are still using their own currency and there are other problems associated with the euro like lack of stabilized interest's rates which might not be suitable for other

member states and there are no incentives for member states to embark on challenging fiscal policies as the EU will protect all members in case of a crisis.

Unworkable inefficient policies.

One of the main problems cited by member states is that nearly half (40%) of its budget is spent on agricultural policies with the result that there is over supply and prices are also regulated. The policies benefited large land-owners rather than eliminating social inequalities.

Problems of net migration.

There are problems of unemployment and overcrowding in some cities caused by free movement of people between member states. There are no controls or regulations which results in inadequate facilities and too much pressure on infrastructure. House prices have gone up in some areas as a result of migration.

Reduced democracy and more bureaucracy.

Local communities' voices have been suppressed as a result as policies and regulations are channeled from the top downwards and there is increased paperwork and administrative duties which cost money too.

Communication barrier as there is no single language among its member states.

All member states speak their own languages and communication at times has hindered progress as member states cannot travel to other member states to find employment as they cannot speak the other member's language.

Control from central no local government decision making powers.

The EU acts like the central government and local governments are rendered powerless as the EU makes laws and policies and channel these to local governments with little or no power to make their own decisions. Some rules can be suitable for one country but equally not good to the other member state.

What are the advantages of remaining in the EU once a member state?

Jobs

To those countries that are already a member state the availability of jobs already created will be a strong argument of staying within the EU. It is estimated that more than three million of the British people work abroad and withdrawal would mean loss of these jobs. Europeans take jobs in Britain which the ordinary British people would otherwise not be bothered doing and leaving the EU would result in a shortage of labour or otherwise Britain has to attract labour from somewhere else.

Guaranteed benefits derived from trade.

The EU is a catalyst and a springboard for economic and business deals between EU member states and the rest of the world. Leaving the EU would mean renegotiating the deals which would be difficult if not imposing. Leaving the EU would mean leaving the world's single market and it would be difficult for other countries to approach a single country first to do business with when there is a ready available market with many benefits. It's common sense that other countries will priorities making business with the EU than any single country. Some investment countries tend to find it easy to invest in countries that are already in the EU and withdrawal would mean loss of such investment.

EU is a dominant force on the negotiating table as it has in the past negotiated major deals with the rest of the world to benefit its member states. It will continue to do so, for example with countries like Canada, China, Japan and the USA. It has made solid business deals and negotiations with the USA to create the largest free trade market. This will open the world's largest market to its members. Leaving the single market will mean a loss to opportunities and investment that will have serious implications on economic development. The EU acts as a catalyst in speeding up development through negotiations and acts as a powerful bargaining force negotiating major deals with the rest of the world.

Exports

Most countries benefit from the EU as it is the largest buyer of its goods and services. The EU is the single market where it's easy to export your goods and services and withdrawal would mean loss of income from exports. Taking the UK for example 50% of its exports are bought in the EU and more than three hundred thousand companies owned by the British are based in EU.

Reduced prices of goods among member states.

Prices of goods and services are cheaper in the EU than anywhere else. A single market means reduced prices of mobile phones for example roaming charges are cheaper within member states than within the rest of the world.

There are other benefits like cheaper flights, easy and cheaper credits cards and finance as the providers are protected by the EU. There are other benefits like easy compensation and insurance services as they are all protected by the EU.

No one country can guarantee such service and withdrawal would be a loss.

Improved living standards, human rights and justice and cleaner environment.

These are among the benefits of remaining in the EU. There are common rules and standards imposed by the EU which other states should follow and implement to the benefit of people of Britain either in home country and when they travel abroad.

The EU as a controller and intermediary to curb and bring big multinational companies to justice.

EU acts as a regulator and advocates for fair competition and prohibits bad practices by multinational companies and advocates for better goods and services by making these multinationals be accountable for their actions. Leaving the EU would mean loss of such protection.

Plenty of opportunities for any single country's inhabitants throughout the EU.

Freedom of movement means plenty of opportunities and benefits for the inhabitants of the member state. There are jobs that can be secured in other member states and learning opportunities as well than might be available in the original member state. This in turn free up pressure on infrastructure in the member state. Taking Britain for example there are 1.4million British people living in other EU member states.

Integration, cooperation and peace.

The main reason of establishing the EU or then EEC was to avoid wars and arguments among Europeans after the second world war. Ever since member states have cooperated, this in turn encouraged peace and prosperity among member states. As one of its main objective, the EU foresees the upholding of peace and human rights throughout Europe and acts as a negotiator and intermediary in resolving conflicts and maintaining peace within member states and throughout the world. It has provided backing and support to all member states. Leaving the EU will leave any country prone to attack and conflicts in the future. No other country will dare attack or come into conflict with its members, there is strength in numbers.

Better working standards and improved pay and working conditions.

The EU tends to impose rules and regulations which every member state must obey and implement and this has meant better living standards and improved wages throughout EU. The EU acts as a regulator and a watchdog or overseer of standards throughout Europe. The EU lays the foundation and acts as a catalyst and negotiator of good deals that benefit the whole region. Any withdrawal would mean a loss of such support and it will be hard or expensive for any single country to come up with similar deals.

Technological research and development.

The EU spends a lot of money on technological and other developments in agriculture that benefit all member states. Taking the 2014-2020 EU budget for example the EU spent 125.6bn euros on development and growth with all member states benefiting from grants and support, and it spent 325bn euros on support for poorer states. Any country would not afford to allocate a lot of money like the EU, to booster growth and development. Taking the UK for example the EU spend a fortune in supporting British farmers, providing grants for university research and a lot of money on boosting jobs in the UK. Withdrawal would mean loss of all these benefits. The UK is the second biggest beneficiary of university grants from the EU having a lot of top universities.

A single point of control.

All member states must abide by the European rules which help bring uniformity to all member states and helps fight crime. Leaving the EU would mean long extradition procedures and delays as it will be difficult to extradite criminals hiding in EU. It tends to eliminate too much bureaucracy among member states as they all have the same laws and procedures.

Loss of the hard work achieved over the years, loss of allies and power to influence future decisions.

Any country leaving the EU would be turning back the clock to the period before joining the EU. There have been great achievements over the years and all EU member states have enjoyed friendship and allies. There had been much advancement in economic and social justice due to the EU. Every member state in the EU had contributed to the development of the EU as a region and to the world as a whole. Leaving would mean turning back the clock and loss of all the things achieved so far for example human rights advancement brought about by the European Union's human rights acts among other acts.

What are the disadvantages of remaining in the EU once a member state?

Cost on membership fees.

Each EU member state contribute a fee to the EU budget, with German being the largest contributor with more than 21.3% of the EU budget contributed in the 2014-2020 budget. The UK contributed up to 12.5% of the budget, France contributed up to 15.7% of the 2014-2024 budget. These membership contributions are in billions per year for example in 2015 according to <u>FULLFACTS</u> the UK contributed £13bn and received a rebate of around £4.5bn that means a net contribution of £8.5bn to the EU budget. Most people would argue that this is not cost effective as they are losing more money with minor benefits. People arguing for the withdrawal from the EU are highlighting that remaining now is a cost. The EU was beneficial in the early years of joining and now the costs outweighs the benefits. Most of the EU's spending is towards agricultural projects with more than 40% being spent towards agriculture and development. Those advanced countries with advanced agricultural technology are finding the fee exorbitant as compared to the benefits they gain.

Too many laws that hinder individual member's progress.

Some member states like Britain argue that most of their small to medium business don't operate in the EU's single market or that the benefits of their inclusion are minimal but they are still governed by the restrictive laws from Brussels which in turn hinder their progress and development.

Continued lack of government control.

Most EU countries have no control of decisions that affects them. The EU passes laws and regulations for all its member states regardless of each countries difference. The laws are passed down from Brussels for all to accept and implement. Some countries feel that they have lost control and their sovereignty as they give up some control and their democratic powers. The world is changing as we know it the EU probably was beneficial in the early years as the countries develop and new technology comes into force more and more governments now see the need to be in control of the decisions they make. This has led other countries to shun the European Union but to keep some of the trade agreements in place.

Lack of proper control of immigration.

During the early years of joining the EU most member states benefited from joining the EU as they filled up the labour shortages quickly, but with the growing number of people from the EU there has been pressure on infrastructure and overcrowding in some areas. The government cannot control population as the EU is a free single market.

Continued lack of proper security.

Foreign criminals can easily travel to one country and another without being traced. The governments cannot properly control their borders. There are no border post people in the EU are freely to come and go and this put the security at risk. Terrorists and other criminals can pose a threat as more and more member states join the EU especially those from the war-torn areas of Syria and Afghanistan.

Most now see the EU as undemocratic and out of date.
Some countries are now thinking of leaving the EU and going alone, they have realized that it's time they do it own their own as the costs are now outweighing the benefits. Some countries like Norway have negotiate or renegotiated some trade and investments trade deals but chose not to bound by the EU's rules and legislations. Remaining will mean a cost as most of the laws are seen as being imposed by individual countries like Germany and France with vested interests which might not be in their best interests. Norway is a good example that leaving or not joining the EU can be beneficial as it is now rich and prosperous. So staying in the EU will only frustrate development and growth of the individual states. As times goes by the EU is becoming less and less favorable and remaining will only help to discourage future prosperity. If other countries cannot join and still trade with the EU and if the benefits are minimal why remain in the EU?
Threat of a lack of future independence and military freedom.
There are growing concerns that the EU in the end will try to form its own army as other countries like Russia and North Korea pose as a threat. This will mean no military freedom of member states as at one point the EU will

control all its member states militarily and economically as the threat grows. The recent influx of refugees from Syria and the Iraq have posed new threats in the form of terrorism hence the need for military army.

Continued lack of fiscal control in the future when faced with economic hardships.
In the future when a country is faced with some fiscal problems it will be difficult to act to correct the problem mainly because of the protection that the EU membership guarantees which hinders incentives for member states to act and try to correct any problems they have in the future. When there is a recession the member states will be unable to combat the recession as they will be unable to loosen its fiscal situation. If the country concerned was not in the EU it would quickly devalue to boost exports which is impossible if in the EU, as all fiscal policies are governed by the EU. The country will be unable to boost jobs through borrowing; it will also be impossible to reduce taxes to combat the deficit.

Why Britain joined the EU did it have anything to do with helping the economy? An overview.
Skepticists insist that the time Britain joined the EU, the EU was in no position to help anyone economically as all its policies were based in agriculture development and fisheries which was minor to the British economy. Why join in 1973 when the EU then EEC was an agricultural and fisheries Community? To answer this question, I will look at the time Britain joined the EEC and the EEC objectives and the political climate at the time of joining.

Firstly, looking at the reasons of rejecting Britain's membership of the EEC in 1963 and 1967 it seems the then president of France Charles de Gaulle seemed to have doubted the willingness and commitment of Britain **politically** to the development and growth of the EU. His reason was that Britain would lead to the breakup of the EEC. The French president Charles de Gaulle a general, thought that Britain had deep seated hostility towards the EEC and joining the EEC would destabilize it. At the time the general also cited the incompatibility of the British economy to the EEC objectives.

The reasons cited by Charles de Gaulle at the time for refusing Britain.

In De Gaulle's very words:

"England in effect is insular, she is maritime, she is linked through her exchanges, her markets, her supply lines to the most diverse and often the most distant countries; she pursues essentially industrial and commercial activities, and only slight agricultural ones. She has in all her doings very marked and very original habits and traditions"

Wikipedia

Clearly the French president highlighted that the British had little agricultural activity and they would not benefit by joining the EEC. The EEC was mainly an agricultural and fisheries community, because of this he was skeptical about the reason why Britain wanted to join.

50 years down the line the British people had realized that they have no gains from joining and wanted out. The French president saw that Britain was independent and its agriculture successful it didn't need any protection then. The EEC was to help countries that were struggling to protect its companies and industries. According to earlier reports it seemed the UK had initially rejected Charles de Gaulle's proposal to join the EEC in favor of making allies with the US. When France and Germany's economies

started to grow then the UK changed their position and decided to join the EEC which was met with skepticism by the then French president. Probably the French president viewed the UK as a Trojan horse for the US. Their economic position was strong and needed not join the EEC. The French president saw UK's stance as there to weaken the EEC and frustrate progress and to represent America's interests. Him being of military background probably he assumed Britain had a political agenda rather than an economic one, Germany and France's economies were gathering momentum and these countries were a threat to peace and security. German and France's growth had nothing to do with the EEC, the growth was due to individual states' effort to stimulating growth through injection of money into the economy. EU policy had always been irrelevant to the economic growth of individual states. At that time Britain had high defense spending overseas that led to continuous balance of payment crises and this balance of payment crises had nothing to do with the fact that Britain was not a member of the EU then EEC.

Having looked at the above reasons for rejecting Britain in the then EEC, it seemed the generals view was skewed, certainly Britain is and was not a puppet of America. Britain had simply foreseen the economic and political opportunities presented by joining the EEC. Britain had seen itself as independent and needed not be governed by the EEC.

Britain joined the EEC because joining was perceived as a way to stop its relative economic decline. Britain's per capita GDP was a third larger than all of the EEC member states in the 1950s. At the time of joining Britain's per capita was now 10% below that of all EEC members.

Joining the EEC has stabilized its per capita GDP since joining the EEC.

Examples from other countries that have withdrawn their European Union membership.

I will look at Article 50 in greater detail in the chapters that follows but here I will just give a brief outline of its role and importance to the EU member states. Any country that joined the EU has the right to withdraw its membership of the EU by invoking Article 50 of the European treaty. This Lisbon treaty gave all the member states an exit clause for those who wanted to withdraw.

"**Article 50**[edit]

1. Any Member State may decide to withdraw from the Union in accordance with its own constitutional requirements.

2. A Member State which decides to withdraw shall notify the European Council of its intention. In the light of the guidelines provided by the European Council, the Union shall negotiate and conclude an agreement with that State, setting out the arrangements for its withdrawal, taking account of the framework for its future relationship with the Union."

Wikipedia

The case of Greenland.

Greenland part of the Danish country left the EU in 1985, initially they had refused to join the EU but because it was part of Denmark they only joined because Denmark had agreed to join. In 1979 Greenland decided to leave the EU when it gained independence and initiated a referendum which was successful as the majority agreed to leave the EEC. In 1985 Greenland left the EEC but it was still governed by other European treaties. The Greenland treaty was introduced to facilitate the withdrawal of Greenland from the treaty by other European communities.

The case of Algeria.

Algeria had joined the EEC since it was a part of France. When it gained independence, it withdrew from the EEC in 1962.

What are the impacts of leaving the EU to the remaining EU block?

EU can start to function properly and realize its full potential, many analysts view Britain as frustrating the development and growth of the EU, Britain refuses to incorporate the single currency notion which is of huge importance and central to the success of the EU's single market. With Britain gone, the EU can start to realize its full potential as it was established with the idea of a single market and with a single currency. The EU will continue to function normally without major changes to its structure or policies, this will be one of the options.

Secondly the EU can make changes to its structure and laws in response to the Brexit to avoid other countries holding referendums in the near future. It will learn from the Brexit and come up with solutions to Brexit's arguments for leaving. The EU will continue to function normally but tries to find common ground to all highlighted problems.

Thirdly I think the EU will have tiers within itself, in other words it can have like the core countries and the periphery countries. The core countries will be responsible for major decision making incorporating all the EU's policies and laws and abiding to all these, whereas the peripheral countries will abide by the EU's policies and laws to a certain degree or by some laws and not the others. The periphery member states will be part of the EU but not incorporate each and every policy and laws.

The other scenario is when there is delegation of power from Brussels to local government member states, in other words a devolution of power to give local governments powers to make rules and laws that affects their countries, with Brussels controlling the overall big policies and regulations. There will be to some extent individual countries sovereign in terms of governance. This is more suited to the current and future of the EU considering the fact that other countries like Turkey, Ukraine and the Balkans would join the EU.

Lastly the EU can become more tighter and more configured as a response to the Brexit. They can nominate a decision-making leader and become more integrated and united than ever before. They can only allow those countries that abides by the EU's rules and policies like the use of a single currency. They can stream down the member states to include those who are serious about the membership and the rules and obligations. The EU can establish its own military army and other services just like in a single country to protect itself from the ever-growing threat of terrorism and refugee influx. They can also prepare themselves in order to deal with threat among itself in form of social tension posed by Christians and Muslims and threat from other countries like Russia. They can form other trading alliances with countries like the USA, currently there are talks to establish the Transatlantic

Trade and Investment(TTI) market that is going to be the world's biggest single or common market.

The last scenario will be the exit of most member states that will destabilize the EU especially looking at concerns that Germany has more power and control as the forming member of the EU. The critics have viewed the EU as serving Germany's own interest. Mistrusts and disagreement for example between France and Germany in handling crises will in the future destabilize the EU. Out of date objectives and goals can mean the collapse of the EU. Unless there have been major reforms to change and modernize the EU to better serve and meet the current needs brought about by the ever-changing factors like terrorism, the EU can collapse as member states exit. How Britain will handle itself after it's exit, and its success thereafter will be among other things a contributing factor to the collapse of the EU in the future. The rise of the populist anti-EU movement in recent years with emphasize on conservatives and national autonomy and sovereignty will see the collapse of the EU in the future if no major reforms are taken by the EU.

Destabilization of the EU and possibility of a chain reaction

Leaving the EU can destabilize the EU, in the first years, uncertainty can cause the EU, problems of growth and development. If unchecked the EU can go into a recession, other countries might follow suit and try to exit the EU thereby initiating a chain reaction with serious consequences to the stability of the EU.

Britain government's views and position in the period leading to the referendum.

A look at the prime minister's stance before the referendum.

The prime minister's views were to remain in the EU and to push for new negotiations and demands until 2017. I can also say that at the moment the vote to leave can be used as a bargaining tool in order for the EU leadership to curve in to the UK's demands. Looking at the proposals put forward by the prime minister it seems the threat of quitting the EU can open doors and allow more bargaining powers. It was Mr. Cameron's stance that individual MP's vote either way they liked, instead of a government's collective stance. Normally the government would urge all the MP's to collectively share the government's view but in this case the prime minister allowed every MP to choose freely how to vote.

The consequences of the Brexit to the stability of the EU can be a factor that will see the EU loosening its grip on cherry picking of its policies and regulations. The UK might be able to strike a new deal as most leaders would want to see Britain remain in the EU.

Immigration as a point of renegotiating the EU membership.

The UK has highlighted the need to control immigration and to curb the benefits they get. The UK government has been proposing for a controlled movement of EU members and the control of the type and benefits they get. The UK has proposed tight controls of its borders, more powers to deport foreign criminals and more control in deciding which benefits Europeans coming here will get and to deport those who cannot find a job within six months. There were proposals that those coming to Britain from the EU have to wait and be resident for four years before they can access any benefits. The government is trying to control and limit the number of Europeans coming to work and claim benefits in Britain.

Delegating decision making powers to London rather than Brussels.

Mr. David Cameron has been advocating for more powers for Britain to make its own laws and rules and not to be governed by the EU. The prime minister hinted that Britain must become more sovereign in the future to decide which course the country will take for example in the case of a recession. The prime minister was proposing that Britain be able through the Bank of England to set up its own fiscal measures and policies rather than let Brussels dictate fiscal measures. Mr. Cameron didn't see the need for Britain to form "ever closer union" with the rest of the EU as the EU recommends, instead he opted for a more sovereign Britain free to decide which course of action the country will take, a country free to make its own laws and not be bound down by Brussels. Mr. Cameron was advocating for the ability of Britain to be able to block EU's legislation which it sees as unfit. Mr. Cameron had vowed to back new legislation giving the UK parliament more powers to block or reject EU's legislation.

Free trade and the ability to make own fiscal policies.

The UK government was advocating for the ability to make their own fiscal and economic policies and regulations that are specific to Britain and implement these rather than adopting the EU's regardless of country differences. In case there is a recession Mr. Cameron was advocating for the British government to be able to deal with the recession itself without the EU imposing restrictions and limiting borrowing capabilities. Mr. Cameron was arguing that most of British people, own their houses and they have mortgages unlike their counterparts in Europe and in case of a recession Britain would be better off making their own fiscal policies rather than let Brussels dictate which course of action to follow. Another argument was that Mr. Cameron saw no need to contribute to the bailout budget in-case other EU members are in recession. The UK government wanted to opt out of this EU's clause. The other point the prime minister made was that Britain wanted to continue to use the sterling rather than adopt the euro as required by the EU.

The other point regarded free trade and competition within the single market.
Britain wanted to safeguard the growth and development of its industries and businesses by advocating for the removal of the red tape and regulations that was unfavorable to the growth and development of its businesses. The prime minister was proposing for the relaxation of Brussels laws and the red tape and the need to encourage growth and development. He wanted to opt out of some of the EU's laws regarding trading in the single market and trading with the rest of the world.

Rejection of a single military army.
Britain rejected the idea of the EU having its own military and security establishments. The EU had proposed the establishment of a military and security army to help protect its borders in the light of the rising

terrorism threat posed by the influx of migrants from Syria and the threat posed by the resurgence of Russia. The influx of immigrants from non-christian countries like Syria Afghanistan and Iraq as refugees has seen a new form of risk and therefore the need for the EU to form its own military to combat such threats, but Britain refused the idea and chose to remain in control of its military and security forces. Britain has not rejected the incorporation of other members like Turkey and the Balkans in the EU but the British government has emphasized the need to control vast migrations from these countries. The idea of the EU is that of a single market where goods, services and people are free to move within a single market without any interference for the single market to realize its full potential. In the light of terrorism and other threats the main question is how will you balance freedom of movement and the provision of security.

Is it easy to strike a balance between freedom of movement within the single market and the ability to be proactive against terrorism and other threats? These are the current threats to the survival of the EU, in the past there was migration of people all Europeans with same values and goals, same religion and the same way of life, but recently countries like Syria and Turkey have been part of the EU directly or indirectly. There has been a huge influx of migration from Islamic states, people who have different views, religion and way of life. This is the major threat to peace and stability within the EU. So, the question is how can you preserve EU's founding principles of free movement, peace, stability and the threats of social tension, terrorism and violence.

Other than the above factors, the UK government was in-line with other EU's policies on equal pay, employment laws, food standards, environment and other human rights laws. Their main argument was that the UK government should have more power to make laws and decisions rather than Brussels channel all authority to London.

Can Britain re hold the referendum in order to stay in the EU? Are there any laws to overrule the referendum results and what can Britain do to remain in the EU if need be?

In the UK, legal system, parliament sets the laws and not the voters so the results are just advisory to the parliament and not mandatory. This means MPs can vote to overturn the decision or new elections can be held and the new party in power will choose to continue with British membership in the EU as part of their campaigning manifesto and if they win the elections it will be a legal requirement or obligation for them to remain in the EU. Britain can renegotiate a deal with the EU to come up with new trade arrangements and for the British governments to select EU policies they want and form new treaties.

Situation before Article 50 of the Lisbon treaty is invoked.

The current feeling in Brussels is that of being late down by Britain, at the current moment there are feelings of anger and disappointment. The EU leaders had hoped that the British people would vote to stay in the EU. The EU is currently facing a lot of challenges and changes at the moment with the recent recessions and global financial crises and the recent migration of refugees from war torn areas like Syria to the European Union. There has been a lot of mistrust and corruption and too much red tape and bureaucracy. There has been divisions and differences, and the exit of Britain is something the leaders don't want at the moment. These are challenging times and the EU survival is being tested, the announcement of the proposed resignation by the British prime minister after the referendum of June 23 2016 is a clear indication of the problems the EU will face in the future. Germany and France were unhappy with the Brexit vote considering there were the founding members. Any exit will threaten the stability of the EU. The EU leaders have called for the immediate invoking of Article 50 of the Lisbon treaty and want Britain to start the exiting process. Any delay can cause a tsunami of exits from the EU as other countries hold referendums to exit the EU. The uncertainty of such a move together with the unknown future can cause destabilization within the EU and cause the EU to go into a recession. The current mood is that of setting Britain as an example to avoid others thinking about exiting the EU as well. The EU leaders are proposing strict and immediate measures to be put in place and to initiate a quick and painful divorce. They are saying that as Britain wants to leave then they should not leave when it suits them, but to leave immediately, by invoking Article 50 of the Lisbon treaty. This is seen as beneficial to the EU which will be able to start its growth and development as a truly single market with a single currency. Other EU members are urging for a soft approach when dealing with the UK and to leave the doors open for the return of the UK. Countries like Poland with vested interests are urging the EU leaders to give Britain time and open more doors for negotiations.

The British government have already selected candidates who are going to run for the prime minister's role in the next elections this year namely Theresa May and Andrea Leadsoms who are both females. The new prime minister will be the one with the responsibility of negotiating the terms and deals of the Brexit and above all the one with the power of invoking Article 50 of the Lisbon treaty.

A look at the economy.

The weeks following the Brexit vote will witness volatile economy and financial markets as uncertainty plays a major role to cause sudden changes in buyers and sellers decisions. A lot of players from small businesses and, multinational companies will react to the news and the market and economy will respond respectively. There will be huge changes in the share prices positively and negatively. There will be financial turmoil around the world with ripple effects. These can be overturned at any time as there can be gains followed by loses and vice versa. The markets and economy are highly unpredictable as a lot of adjustments are made. Many people will try to avoid loses and making gains and adjust accordingly. There would be gains in the British pound as world markets tumble and there could be loses in the British pound with gains in the rest of the world. Many problems can be laying ahead, David Cameron's decision to resign can have negative influence in the bargaining decision making process with Brussels and weaken Britain's standing with the rest of the world. The new prime minister might not be experienced enough to handle negotiations and make deals with the EU that can positively affect the economy as people become more uncertain. The economy responds more to people's perceptions rather than actual facts; an inexperienced prime minister can be viewed as a weakness in the bargaining process and lose the upper hand posing a risk and introducing uncertainty in the markets and the markets can become volatile. The EU leaders are calling for a hard stance with regard to Britain to try and discourage further tsunami effects which will destabilize the EU. Companies with headquarters abroad will leave and relocate elsewhere, investment will be cut short or relocated elsewhere making Britain less favorable for business.

British companies and businesses will still have access to the single market and few weeks or months after the results the market will stabilize and as negotiations of various treaties and packages continue the economy can have gains and losses. The main thing that will be greatly affected will be future investment and the balance of payments deficit. Britain will have to negotiate as soon as possible trade deals with the rest of the world to boost the economy and further development. After the election of prime minister David Cameron's successor then and there will the economy starts to stabilize. Most of the commotion in the economy will be due to uncertainty, a ship without a captain is a cause of much concerns and worries. When the new prime minister will be in place then the peoples' worries and uncertainty will easy up. The pound will increase vis-a-vis that of the rest of the world. Things might improve although not as much as when the vote was to remain. Most of the economy will depend on how swiftly the government will respond to changes and other influences. Most also depends on what will happen to the rest of the EU. If there are other exits or referendum or instability you might actually see Britain's economy improving. There are a lot of factors altogether but in short any turmoil within the EU and the rest of the world might actually fuel growth of the British economy.

Foreign Investment.

The period after Brexit might see a decline in foreign investment as uncertainty and fear cause people to panic and withdraw or withhold plans to invest in Britain. It is likely that direct foreign investment will decline after Brexit until negotiations are held between the EU and the UK. As long as there is uncertainty as to what is going to happen any kind of investment will be to some extend minimal. But looking at the overall picture Britain can still forge new relationships with other countries to quickly boost the economy. It all depends on how quickly the British government will react, are they going to take their opportunities and attract investments from somewhere else. Investors invest in Britain not simply because Britain has access to the single market, so in or out of the EU will not stop others investing in the UK. After Brexit, there will be initial disruption of direct foreign investment until that time when trade deals are negotiated. Currently half of Britain's foreign investment is from other EU member states. In the world, only China and the US receives more foreign investment than the UK. Multinationals sees Britain as attractive because it is part of the EU, there are reduced costs in terms of tariffs and duties to be paid, hence the multinationals can find it cheaper to export to other countries from the UK. Car industries and financial institutions like banks invest in Britain because it is part of the EU, it's easy to move resources and services across the EU. These will be hit if Britain exit the EU. Uncertainty over the future of Britain in the EU will affect enormously direct foreign investment, the EU membership reduces costs of trade and investment which makes the member countries attractive for investment. With a large pool of educated labour force, use of English language and a good rule of law Britain has been seen as a hot spot for investment. Exiting the EU will mean more tariffs and costs so industries in the UK after the exit like the car industry will be hit because it will be expensive to export to other EU members. Most multinational companies' headquarters are outside the UK, and these multinationals find it easy to relocate in any EU member country because it is cheaper, in terms of reduced costs, and tariffs. It's easy to coordinate activities, staff, services and skills between headquarters and the local company. If UK leaves the EU, then coordination and costs will increase. The car manufacturing in the UK will fall as foreign car manufacturing industries will relocate elsewhere or reduce production in the UK, for example BMW will find it expensive to manufacture cars in the UK and export these to other EU countries. Prices of cars in the UK will increase as imported cars will be costly due to tariffs and custom duties as UK will no longer be in the EU.

The UK can join the European Free Trade Agreement to offset the impact of exiting the EU, this will still guarantee them access to the single market with little tariffs and duties to pay. In this case the only additional cost will be from headquarters to local company costs. Even if the UK leaves the EU and joins the EFTA the UK car industry will still be hit as car production will be relocated elsewhere.

In short Brexit, will have negative impact on foreign investment until such time the UK is able to secure agreements like joining the EFTA or to seek new trade agreements with other countries like China, Canada, India, Russia, Australia and the US.

Situation 2 years after implementation of Article 50 of the Lisbon Treaty.

The invoking of Article 50 of the Lisbon treaty will signal the exit of Britain from the EU. The Lisbon treaty paves the way for the end of a relationship between the EU and Britain. This is the first time the Article has been used since the formation of the EU. In the treaty, it is advised that it takes or should take two years for any country to withdraw from the EU but there are a lot of negotiations to be made which will make it impossible for Britain to exit the EU in two years. Such negotiations will take several years. Each member state has to make deals and agree on some terms regarding Britain. Other members might want to forge other agreements to safe guard rights of people from their country working and living in Britain. Normally it takes a lot more time for any negotiations with the EU. It also depends with the mood with the EU leaders whether they will try and accommodate the Britain and adopt a soft approach or they will take a hard stance. The mood at the moment is that the four big EU players namely, Germany, France, Finland and the Dutch are calling for a tough stance towards Britain, they are objecting to any negotiations. If this is the way things will go, then the processes will be shorter than expected.

Critics argue that Britain will find it hard to secure trade deals outside European Union. It seems each and every major country on earth is working hard to secure trade deals with the EU so why the UK is severing its ties with the EU.

EU- Canada deal.

The EU is currently negotiating a trade deal with Canada, the Comprehensive Economic and trade Agreement (CETA) that would have added 1.3bn to the UK's economy if it had not voted to exit. If the UK have gone it alone it would be impossible for the UK to strike such a deal alone with Canada. The EU has a lot of bargaining power which makes it easy to strike deals with the rest of the world. The EU- Canada deal has already been signed but only awaits some modifications. This deal could have added nearly 30% to the value of UK's trade business had it not opted out of the EU.

The EU-South Korean deal.

The EU struck a deal with the South Korean government that has helped all EU member states. The agreement was expected to boost bilateral trade agreement between the EU and South Korea. After the deal was signed exports from the UK to South Korea grew by almost half. Only after the deal did exports to South Korean reach their highest-level amounting to more than £6bn. If Britain exit the EU, there would be reduced exports to South Korea and the UK has to make a new trade agreement with South Korea that can take years to negotiate. In 2016 EU exports to South Korea increased by 55% which benefits every EU member, and EU member companies saved altogether nearly 2,8bn euros in scrapped taxes and tariffs which is a big boost to the economy and EU businesses. Leaving the EU would mean a loss of such savings and alone I don't think Britain will be able to make such savings.

Transatlantic Trade and Investment Agreement (TTI)between EU and America.

The idea is to promote trade and economic growth between the USA and the EU. The agreement focuses on market access, regulations and some cross-border protection and cooperation. The agreement is seen as a way to boost the EU's economy by more than 120bn euros and the USA's economy by more than 90bn euros. Leaving the EU would mean less trade for Britain with the US in the future. Britain has to strike its own new deal with the US which cannot be as favorable as that of the TTI.

There are other trade deals between the EU and the rest of the world like Singapore, Japan, New Zealand and Australia which all if completed and signed would contribute 88% more to the UK's trade. The EU have big bargaining powers providing access to the world's markets. The Japan and the US deals alone if completed would provide the UK with access to two thirds of the worlds market. The strength of the EU is that it normally signs comprehensive deals that covers a lot of areas and which bring a lot of benefits to its member states.

Each and every major country at the moment is looking to sign a deal with the EU to increase its trade deals, in theory it seems the UK will lose much of its trade in terms of exports and imports to the EU. But it might take time to secure trade agreements to replace those already negotiated by the EU. A lot has to be done by the UK government to secure trade deals before it fully exits the EU.

Complete exit without any more special ties with the EU. Scenario One.

After the two years, had passed assuming that Britain left the EU without any renegotiations, I would think that Britain will forge other trade deals with the rest of the world. There are other players who would want to take this crisis as an opportunity to strike trade deals with Britain namely, Russia, China, India, the US, New Zealand, Canada, Australia and the rest of the world.

The UK has to refocus its entire approach in order to attract foreign investment and increase growth and development. They have to restructure their growth and development plans. They have to appoint new people and set up new positions and structures geared to the attraction of foreign investment and to stimulate growth and development. A committee or group of specialist people can be set up with the aim of pooling resources to find ways of stimulating growth and attracting much needed foreign investments. New posts will be created in order to speed up the process. Funds should be set aside to help this operation. A committee of specialist people will be sent to other countries to pave way for trade deals and investment opportunities.

The UK will no longer have access to the single market, now it had to negotiate it's own deals with the rest of the world. Now it will be paying tariffs and custom duties to trade with EU members. It can strike deals by joining the European Free Trade Agreement as in the case of Norway but still pay a small duty to trade with European traders. The UK will have made trade deals with countries like India, China, US, Canada and the commonwealth countries.

Possible trade deals with India, China, Canada and the US.

India is the third largest foreign investor in the UK accounting for £16bn of investment in 2015. There are 12 Indian companies operating in the UK at the present moment employing up to 110 000 people and after two years there will be trade deals and more companies operating in the UK. At the moment, a delegate had been sent to India to look for trade opportunities in the wake of the Brexit. Britain will take advantage of the already special relationship with India to try and attract more foreign investment. The UK needs this foreign investment in order to offset its balance of payment deficit. China, Canada and the US are other major players investing in the UK. There are a lot of opportunities and business deals that can be made especially that now Britain has left the EU. Even deals that were less favorable in the past can seem lucrative now that the UK is no longer part of the EU. The government in the initial phase will try and secure as much deals as possible to offset the gap left by the loss of access to the single market. We can see more deals being made outside of Europe mainly within the commonwealth. It might also be advantageous to initiate trade talks as the process might be faster with less bureaucracy and delays. The need to offset the balance of payments deficit will mean less waste of time negotiating deals. At this stage and point in time it's half a loaf is better than nothing. Britain will be under pressure to perform, under pressure to secure the much-needed foreign investment and above all pressure from Brussels will Britain throw everything to avoid the I told you so from EU leaders. Any failure will put smiles on the EU leaders and the whole world is watching whether the British have been daft or not. Most people in Brussels, considering the current feelings of anger and dismay, will be hoping that Britain stumble on its knees and beg to be taken back by the EU. The British system and way of life can be a factor in deciding whether they are going to make it or not. Much reforms and ambitious projects have to be established and implemented if Britain is to see it through.

Exit from the EU but with some renegotiated trade deals.

The UK can leave the EU but strike trade deals that allows itself to access the single market at a fee as in the case of Norway. If they decide to go this route it seems there won't be enough savings in the contributory fee they pay, because Norway is paying what the UK is paying now as a way of contributing to the EU's budget in exchange of access to the free market. The only gains would be in terms of having Britain as a sovereign country not governed by the EU. Economically depending on other factors like more secured trade agreements outside the EU, Britain can make it and can manage to attract the much-needed foreign investment. It can choose to adopt some treaties which it sees fit and ignore some that are not ideal for its growth and development. Britain can join other establishments like the Economic Trade Area to compensate for the loss of the EU membership and still trade within the single market. People from the EU can still work and live in Britain after the agreement or it can decide the course of action to take and impose conditions on movement of travel and access to benefits. The EU leaders can object to the demands of the UK and refuse to restrict movement as in the case of Swiss where because of restricted movement of people and goods, now the EU is threatening to freeze and suspended some of the services to Swiss.

The UK can still negotiate a lot of bilateral arrangements in exchange of access to the single market, instead of joining the EEA it can join the European Free Trade Association (EFTA)which has different rules but still allows one access to the single market. This will allow the UK to choose some agreements that are considered as beneficial to the UK economy and leave the rest and will still make a financial contribution towards the budget of the EFTA. In this case the UK will not be obliged to apply all EU laws and regulations but will still have to implement some agreements that allows free trade and movement of goods and services.

The main problems with the above scenarios is that the UK will choose to cherry pick what it desires from the EU's policies and choose to ignore all the unwanted policies. Such a move is unfavorable with EU leaders as they will not allow such a move otherwise that will result in the collapse of the EU. The EU leaders were recently been angry as in the case of the Swiss where it agreed to Honor all agreements and allow free movement of people but later chose to impose restrictions. The EU responds to such a move was to freeze and suspend the agreed trade agreements between the Swiss and the EU.

The Third Scenario: The UK has only a customs agreement with the EU.

This is the case with other countries like Turkey where it has customs and tariffs agreement with the EU and agreements to impose the EU's regulations and tariffs to all products it exports. In return it can freely export to the EU single market, without paying any tariffs, taxes or custom duties. But this route is normally taken by those countries that wants to join the EU but they are still preparing in order to meet the entry requirements. There is no access to trade services and financial institutions which account for nearly 80% of UK's trade and because of this this is highly unlikely scenario to find Britain in.

Article 50 of the Lisbon treaty.

This Lisbon treaty agreement enables a country to withdraw its membership from the EU by notifying the EU of its intent formally by invoking Article 50. After two years, the country that wants to withdraw will cease to be a member of the EU unless if all the other members agree to extent the period after the two years has expired. The main advantage is that a country will give notice of its intent to leave the EU in which the EU leaders have to act upon and negotiate terms of leaving, strike new deals and negotiate new trade agreements with the country concerned. The advantages of the Lisbon treaty are that firstly, that it is a guaranteed way of leaving the EU, once the article is invoked there is no turning back. After the two-year period, has expired the country concerned will no longer be part of the EU. Secondly the advantage of the treaty is that once invoked it triggers negotiations straight away with the EU leaders meeting with the rest of the 27 members to discuss the way forward.

The disadvantages of the Article are that it's a one-way street because once invoked there is no turning back. It's a sure way of leaving the EU with or without negotiating a better trade deal, at the end of the two years if no extension is allowed then you must leave the EU. The other disadvantage is that once invoked the life of the other country will be in the hands of the the remainder members of the EU and the country concerned ceases to have any say in the withdrawal process. The outcome might mean a less favorable trade agreement for the exiting country as the EU leaders might take a protection stance to discourage other member states from leaving thereby punishing the country that's exiting. This is the current feeling with the EU leaders they are angered by the UK's decision to leave the EU, that they want to take a tough stance, and refuse a soft approach towards Britain.

The EU can block membership to other establishment like membership to the Free Trade Agreement. They can put strict requirements to discourage the country concerned and any other members who might be thinking of leaving. The last disadvantage is that the timetable will be in the hands of the EU leaders rather than that of the exiting country.

The UK can avoid the Article 50 process by unilateral agreement by repealing the 1972 European community act. It could recite the Vienna convection as a way of leaving the EU. It seems any country can withdraw from the treaty unilaterally and article 50 is there to guide the EU and to make it easy for the leaving country to negotiate new trade deals. The only drawback to this process would be that the EU will be left with no option to negotiate with the exiting country therefore it will be in their right to refuse any other trade agreements. This unilateral process will be like the automatic termination of any membership without any room for negotiations.

Situation 5years after implementation of Article 50 of the Lisbon Treaty.

The UK might still be in the EU 5 years after invoking of Article 50 of the Lisbon treaty, this is because this is the first time a country has invoked article 50. There are a lot of trade agreements to be renegotiated with all the 27 remaining countries of the EU. The process is cumbersome and takes years to complete. Most trade deals have taken over many years to reach and complete. The Canadian-EU deal has been ongoing for more than 7years. The renegotiations might take years to complete and the 2 years' framework offered by the Lisbon treaty is just a guideline. Brussels have powers to extend such period as it sees it fit. I think the EU leadership at the moment is taking a hard stance on Brexit in order to maintain EU'S stability by discouraging other member states from wanting to exit as well through holding of referendums.

Britain could still be guided by EU's policies and regulations and to what extent just depends on progress in negotiations and the success of other trade deals. In five years' time Britain, might have renegotiated another favorable trade agreement with the EU and decides to remain in the EU. I think the EU might allow the UK to cherry pick some of the policies and regulations it wants as long as they contribute towards the EU's budget. The political climate is changing, especially with the rise of the populist or euro skeptic movement which is anti-EU, I think the EU will reform and try also to change with the times and try to accommodate the demands of countries like Swiss and Britain.

The situation Britain would be in depends on several factors, firstly considering that it has left the EU, but has renegotiated trade deals with the EU and has deregulated its economy and trade. Now that it fully trades with the rest of the world with countries like China, Canada and

Russia and has established and supported attraction of foreign investment. Then GDP can be expected to grow with more than 1% a year. In this case the only changes would be in terms of sovereignty and movement of people to some extent. In this case I will assume that the UK's GDP will be higher than if the country had stayed in the EU. This is because now Britain will have freedom to trade with other countries, freedom to secure new investments and new trade agreements but still having access to the single market. Although it will be contributing towards the EU's budget, there is a lot of deregulation and removal of the red tape and too much bureaucracy that are now stifling growth and development. The country will be able to attract investment from elsewhere. The country can impose work permit rules to attract only skilled workers rather than anyone from the EU, and that will abate growth and development.

The second case is when the UK has failed to secure any trade deals with the EU and fails to attract any form of investment from the rest of the world. In this case I would assume than GDP will fall by more than 2% and Britain will be in a worse situation than if it had remained in the EU. Britain might find it hard to do deals with the rest of the EU and the rest of the world. Britain after withdrawal can be unattractive to investment simply because it will be costly to invest in the country. Exports will be expensive as well as imports as they will no longer be in the EU where there are no tariffs. The EU at the moment is striking major deals with the rest of the world, in recent years it had made big deals with Japan, South Korea, Singapore, Canada, and the USA, almost with every single major country. I would think that most countries would opt to trade with the EU rather than the UK, because with the EU there will be a lot of savings as 27 countries are better than one country.

Even if the UK manages to secure trade deals with the rest of the world especially commonwealth countries, it can still face problems, as these low-cost countries can present stiff competition and make British firms vulnerable to competition.

Situation 10 years after implementation of Article 50 of the Lisbon Treaty.

According to Open Europe's Brexit report Britain's GDP could be lower by 2,2% in 2030 if the EU refuse to trade with Britain and if it fails to secure other trading partners. If Britain prefers to deregulate and avoids protectionism, then it could be better off on 6.8% of GDP that is if it negotiates trade agreements with EU and the rest of the world. Britain can follow other countries like Swiss and the Norway and renegotiates trading deals with EU and establishes other links with the rest of the world. The Norway and the Swiss are not governed by the EU yet they have established trading agreements together and still trades with the EU. Although the Norway and Swiss cases are different to the British case, Britain can borrow and adapt their policies to suit Britain. Norway is not a member state of the EU, but is linked to the EU through the European Economic Area. Norway because of the EEC membership is only governed by 21% of the EU laws which means it's as good as free as compared to other EU member states. The EU is Norway's biggest trade partner accounting for 91.8bn euros in 2008 of trade mainly energy supplies and the EU exporting nearly 44bn euros of exports to Norway.

The Norwegian parliament make all laws and legislation without any interference from the EU. Norway still benefits from the presence of a free market with free movement of goods and services without the need to pay taxes and custom duties. This has made Norway a rich national which is sovereign and uncontrolled by the EU. Norway can still participate in the EU contributing to legislation laws, for example in security and defense.

The Swiss case is similar to the Norwegian case; they both are free from controls by the EU yet they are biggest trading partners with the EU. The Swiss negotiated some treaties with the EU to trade even though they were not governed by the EU laws. The Swiss negotiated up to ten agreements that facilitated development and free access to the single market.

Just like the two cases above Britain can still make meaningful treaties with the EU to continue accessing the free market. The Swiss have their own currency but the euro is still accepted in some areas because the Swiss is surrounded by nations that use the euros. Britain can pay a small fee as compared to the current contribution fee which is in billions to safe guard continued vested interests in the EU.

If Britain decided to go it alone there are advantages to this, the UK will be able to deregulate and increase its competitiveness without much interference from Brussels. The parliamentary sovereignty will be restored as the government will be able to make laws themselves than let Brussels dictate to them. The British government will be able to take control of the immigration process and limit the number of people coming to leave and work in the UK. The British government will be able to formulate a trade policy that will make it less expensive to import from other countries at the same time improving exports to other countries. The policies will aim to boost growth and development through various trade agreements. The government of Britain will be able to replace and modify European laws to suit local people's interest and get the local people involved in the decision-making process rather than let Brussels tell them what they can do or should not do. The UK government will reduce or eliminate altogether the contribution they make towards the EU budget and be able to use the money somewhere else. To sum up the main idea in this scenario is for Britain to gain much needed independence from the control of Brussels at any cost. In reality this has nothing to do with trade but with avoiding the burden of being told what to do and what you cannot do. It's about liberation from being dictated to on what to do rather than anything else. This is about removing the red tape and doing without too much bureaucracy. In this case the UK can rely on the World Trade Organization's rules to do its trade with the rest of the world. It will gain a lot of freedom from the EU and will be able to control its own trade policy.

What is the future of the EU post Britain?

Britain refused to use the euro currency, the euro had been a disaster with high unemployment rates

Most people argue that the EU will operate fully if all countries were a super-state with one currency

circulating. They view Britain's presence as hindering progress and development as it has refused to use the euro currency. But on the other side Britain has seen the weakness of the euro currency, the rising unemployment, inflation and recession in member states using the euro, and because of this among other reasons there are now strong arguments to leave. People believe that remaining in the EU now will only frustrate the development of the EU, Britain refused the use of the euro, there are now strong arguments that leaving the EU will help the EU find its destiny as they will be prosperous as a single currency state. Britain not being part of the euro currency has made the EU fail to take proper control of its institutions that has hindered progress. Once Britain has withdrawn the EU will become a unified state this will allow the EU to grow faster as it will be easy to implement its policies as a unified state.

Britain believes it gained by being in the EU but there are no more gains to be made and it's time to leave.

The EU might severe any links with Britain just to make it an example so that others will not try to exit the EU. Germany and France have been encouraging the quick exit of Britain and the quick invoking of Article 50 of the Lisbon treaty. They have seen Britain's exit as not good to the EU as a whole, they conceded that Britain's exit would destabilize the EU and therefore a quick divorce from the EU was eminent. The EU's top leaders have taken a strict stance on Britain and they are urging it to leave as soon as possible and they have not left any room for any future renegotiations. They argued that any delay will prolong uncertainty and cause problems within the EU. Their main argument is that Britain must act quickly in order for the EU to avoid a chain reaction. Other member states like Poland are indirectly in favor of Britain's stance as they highlighted that the EU is now untrustworthy and undemocratic. There are mixed feelings across Europe and fears as well especially considering the Greece crises.

There had been suggestions that Britain can follow the Norway or Swiss option and decides to pay a fee for being part of the EU, that will enable renegotiations and form some treaties without much government control from Brussels.

Will Britain join again the EU in the future and what will be likely impact of such a move.

Britain can still rejoin the EU, but it seems it has to do everything from scratch, it has to negotiate everything from start with EU leaders without any favours or rebates.

Britain in the future might rejoin the EU, depending with who is in power and which political party is ruling the country at the time. I think the EU leaders will leave doors open to try and avoid chain reactions in the future and the destabilization of the EU. At the current moment, it is highly unlikely that the doors will be left open. The EU leaders have taken a tough stance on Britain to avoid other member states following Britain's footsteps. The Germans and the French are campaigning for a tough stance on Britain. They want Britain out as fast as possible, their argument being that, Britain decided to leave and therefore leave means leave. They are calling for Britain to initiate Article 50 of the Lisbon treaty as soon as possible. They want a quick amicable divorce so they can start to build the EU post Britain as soon as possible. The uncertainty of Britain's exit will destabilize the EU. At the moment, other few member states with vested interests like Poland have urged the EU leaders to take it easy on Britain, they are proposing that Britain be given enough time to exit and the doors be left in case they hold another referendum to remain.

But personally, I think Britain should move forward, adjust and adapt to the changing world. A lot of successful countries are not in the EU yet they are rich and prosperous. Other European countries have survived without being a member state of the EU, namely Norway and Swiss. Britain never needed EU and or even if they did that was in the early years after joining, now the benefits are minimal. Look at the pressure on infrastructure, unemployment levels, social tensions and crime rates. The people of Britain have voted; the results reflects the majority of the people's feelings. Looking at the results and the geographical distribution of the votes a clear picture can be seen that the British people want out of EU like yesterday. Any political party that wants to stay in power must abide by the people's choices. A quick look at the results shows that those areas with people who voted to stay in the EU have greater numbers of immigrants or are further to the north in Scotland. The real British people especially the old generations have voted to exit the EU. Immigrants are a minority as compared to the local people, and any party that's serious about politics will take the results seriously and try to accommodate the people's wishes in their policies.

There has been a lot of talks about holding another referendum in case the results are over turned, but would that be fair? What about the rights of those who have voted to leave? Would that be democratic that if you get a result which you don't want then you call for a second referendum? I think in the future, considering the mood at the time, it will take time and a different political party for Britain to start thinking about a return to the EU. As far as the conservatives are concerned and still in power I would say the results truly reflects the will of the people. The capital city's inhabitants have voted to remain in the EU, nevertheless they don't represent the entire population of Britain. There must be a shift of power for anyone to consider returning back in the EU and as long as the conservatives are in power I think it will take years for Britain to consider rejoining the EU again. The only way forward for now and the future is for Britain to form close associations with the EU and the rest of the world. Britain has to try and maintain aspects of their policies which are in line with those of the EU. Britain has to maintain good trade relationships with the EU as a partner and not a member. They must renegotiate a new trade agreement without being governed by the EU. The feelings in Brussels are of anger and dismay over Britain but in the future, the door might be left open for the return to being a member or just a trading partner. Even Brussels know that democratic voting systems are unpredictable, and the resigning of major players in London like the prime minister opens doors for future talks with Brussels with whomever will be in power then. The people have voted and to be re-elected any party must consider the will of the people; they must listen and act upon the people's wishes.

The exit of Britain might signal the future of the EU. Britain's exit might actually signal the exit of other countries in EU and the collapse of the EU unless the EU reforms itself to meet changing political climate. The EU has been blamed as undemocratic and lost in touch, their policies were geared to solve the problems of the early 70's and early 90's. The EU need to reform and keep up with the current political, social and economic climate if it must remain in existence.

Why would Britain want to join the EU again in the future?

First looking back at the main reasons Britain joined the EU in the early 1970s, Britain was having a balance of payments deficit due to overseas spending on defense. Britain was successful agriculturally and industrially, it had good trade links with the rest of the world but was spending a lot of money on defense that caused balance of payment deficit. This in turn caused a continuous decline in GDP from 1945 to 1972 relative to other EU members. However, after joining the EU it's economy was relatively stable between 1972 to 2010, it had a GDP of around 15% more than the EEC members in the 1950s and by the time it joined the EU it's GDP was 2% less than the EEC members. In light of this, other theorists argue that Britain joined the EU to curb its economic decline. The difference in GDP per capita between Britain and the six founding EU members was more than 15% in the 1950, around 10% in the 1960 and 2% in 1972 just before they joined.

Dealing with the aftermath shock if uncontrolled that will result in a recession.

Looking at the aftermath of Brexit, initially there are going to be a lot of uncertainties, that will plunge the economy into a chaos if proper action is not taken up quickly. Changes means Britain will have to deal with a shock in the economy and be prepared for a recession the severity or magnitude and the length will depend on what action the leaders will take.

The IMF and the Governor of England have all talked about a shock in the economy as Britain withdraw from the EU. As Britain prepares to exit the EU some businesses will cancel their investments, consumer confidence will fall and Britain might end up in a recession. There will be a lot of business uncertainty and investment levels might fall to low levels due to this uncertainty and withdrawal of multinational companies, foreign banks etc. Skills and innovation might actually become a problem unless the government comes up with a national plan to boost investment and plug the skills gap from the rest of the world.

The IMF has warned that Britain will plunge into a recession if no corrective action is taken quickly to prevent it. Exiting the EU will affect British living standards and inflation will go up. Stock markets can fall although there might recover soon after-wards but the housing market might actually be affected bringing house prices down. The other downside is that Britain can be left hanging with a lot of trade agreements that it will not be able to terminate as soon as possible but which it might still be obliged to honor.

Looking at the accounting books, it seems Britain has a record current accounting deficit which makes it unfavorable as a trading partner with the rest of the world. That alone can increase fears of recovery if the country falls into a recession. Britain's industry might initially contract, spending power will drop and business investment will drop as well all which will make the economy shrink unless big steps are taken to correct the issue. In 2015 Britain had a record current account deficit of around 7% of GDP, which means huge steps must be taken in order to start the recovery of the economy. This deficit reflects a big trade gap with the rest of the world. The Bank of England has highlighted that in the past it was easy to close the account deficit because of huge foreign investment from the EU, Britain's major foreign investor.

Weak trading links with the rest of the world would only mean the widening of the account deficit gap estimated to be 21bn by next year. The main reason being that foreign investors would be uncertain and will not take risks of investing or holding Britain's investments, this will result in the loss of investments which will in turn widen the account deficit or the balance of payments. Britain is paying more money as dividends and other payments than what it is receiving from foreign investments. In the future, there could be higher interest rates which will affect mortgage payers and businesses and there could be credit crunch.

More measures needed to be taken as soon as possible to avoid the country going into a recession and the economic decline associated with it. More trade links with other countries like China and the rest of the world must be setup. If uncontrolled there will be continuous economic decline, and the only way they are going to stop this decline is to rejoin the EU or negotiate other trade deals to still access the single market and trade.

Leaving the EU means that Britain will have to negotiate its own trade deals missing out on big opportunities like the Transatlantic Trade and Investments market (TTI), which is a single market that is currently being negotiated by the EU and the United States of America. Leaving the EU means that Britain will no longer have rights to excess the TTI, the world's biggest market. It will have to renegotiate its own trade deals which can be difficult. All this will make Britain want to rejoin the EU in the future. Fears of security can make Britain want to rejoin the EU in the future. Politically it's safe to be part of the 28 than to do it alone. Any future political instability can mean security risk to Britain, every country needs allies and backup. If it's going to war, protecting borders, dealing with insurgency I think it will be ideal if it's in partnership with another country or the EU than for Britain to do it all alone.

Political threats from other countries.

Threats from other countries or even the EU itself in the future after the exit can make Britain reconsider its position and rejoin the EU. Although some can argue that the threat of terrorism will actually prohibit such a move considering the notions of open borders and free movement, I will emphasize that being part of EU or not that will not stop terrorism. Terrorist have operated in other countries and there is the threat of home grown terrorists which has nothing to do with whether Britain is still part of the EU or not. So, threats from the EU itself, other countries like Russia or North Korea or China or the USA in the distance future can make Britain want to rejoin the EU, although the idea is remote at the time of writing.

To conclude they say fortune favours the brave!

Remember Fortune favours
the Brave

Best Wishes Brexit